Alberto Bandeira
Antônio Vitor Machado
Patrício B. Maracajá

# Ethno-knowledge in the use of Medicinal Plants in the 14th region of EMATER-PB

Alberto Bandeira
Antônio Vitor Machado
Patrício B. Maracajá

# Ethno-knowledge in the use of Medicinal Plants in the 14th region of EMATER-PB

**Ethno-knowledge of the use of Medicinal Plants in the 14th Administrative Region of EMATER-PB**

ScienciaScripts

**Imprint**

Any brand names and product names mentioned in this book are subject to trademark, brand or patent protection and are trademarks or registered trademarks of their respective holders. The use of brand names, product names, common names, trade names, product descriptions etc. even without a particular marking in this work is in no way to be construed to mean that such names may be regarded as unrestricted in respect of trademark and brand protection legislation and could thus be used by anyone.

Cover image: www.ingimage.com

This book is a translation from the original published under ISBN 978-620-2-19136-4.

Publisher:
Sciencia Scripts
is a trademark of
Dodo Books Indian Ocean Ltd. and OmniScriptum S.R.L publishing group

120 High Road, East Finchley, London, N2 9ED, United Kingdom
Str. Armeneasca 28/1, office 1, Chisinau MD-2012, Republic of Moldova, Europe
Printed at: see last page
**ISBN: 978-620-7-69952-0**

# SUMMARY

# SUMMARY

Ethnobotany deals with the study of the knowledge and conceptualizations developed by any society about the plant world, encompassing both the way a social group classifies plants and how they use them. On the other hand, in a broad sense, Ethnoveterinary can be conceptualized as the science that preserves and values the knowledge of popular practices used to treat and prevent diseases that affect animals. It is likely that the use of medicinal plants as medicines is as old as man himself, and is more evident in developing countries, where most of the poor population does not have access to pharmaceutical medicines. The general aim of this study was to assess ethno-knowledge about the use of medicinal plants in the municipalities that make up the 14$^a$ Administrative Region of the Paraiba State Technical Assistance and Rural Extension Company, based in the city of Pombal, in the Paraíba sertão. The study was carried out using a descriptive field study with a qualitative approach. A previously structured questionnaire containing objective and subjective questions was used as a data collection tool. It was found that over 90% of those interviewed use medicinal plants to treat human illnesses and over 60% use this type of treatment in conjunction with bee honey. The plants most used by the interviewees were: lemon balm, macela, lavender, holy grass, mastruz and mint. Most of the interviewees said they used honey from Africanized bees. The medicinal plants used to treat diseases in humans were cured by an average of over 90% of those interviewed. The average use for animals was 50% and the average use of medicinal plants associated with honey was 48%.

Keywords: Ethno-knowledge. Medicinal plants. Use in humans and animals.

# 1  INTRODUCTION

The use of plants for medicinal purposes is a very old practice, dating back to the origins of humanity, when man began to better understand the environment around him. As he got to know the plant species, he discovered what to use them for and how to use them, both as food and for medicinal purposes.

This preliminary knowledge was passed down from generation to generation. And as time went by, more information was added to it. This gave rise to what is now known as ethno-knowledge, which consists of the passing on of information about, mainly, the use of plant species in the treatment of certain ailments of a chronic or non-chronic nature.

On the other hand, when man selected the first plant species that could be used medicinally, he found that many of them could also be used to treat certain diseases that affected animals. Thus, although Ethnoveterinary is an independent branch of ethno-knowledge, it is closely related to Ethnobotany.

It is important to point out that despite the advances made in Pharmacology due to the development of Biotechnology, the use of medicinal plants is one of the few activities developed by man in ancient times that is still used today.

The general aim of this study is to evaluate ethno-knowledge regarding the use of medicinal plants in the municipalities that make up the 14ª Administrative Region of Emater-PB, based in the city of Pombal, in the Paraíba state.

In order to achieve this objective, a bibliographical survey was initially carried out to show the emergence and evolution of Ethnobotany and Ethnoveterinary, where it was possible to demonstrate that despite advances in the medical sciences, medicinal plants are still widely used by the population, especially in underdeveloped countries.

However, given the recognized value of medicinal plants, their use has been encouraged by the World Health Organization itself. In Brazil, their use is also encouraged by the Ministry of Health, which has already set up a specific program in this area.

Ethnoveterinary, like ethnobotany, is widely used throughout the world. In Brazil, it is used in all regions of the country and is seen as one of the alternatives to the high prices charged for veterinary medicines.

It should be emphasized that the ethnobotanical and ethnoveterinary data needed for this study was collected in the municipalities of Cajazeirinhas, Condado, Coremas, Lagoa, Paulista, Pombal, São Bentinho, São Domingos and Vista Serrana, which are part of the assistance hub defined by Emater-PB for its 14$^a$ Administrative Region, using a previously structured questionnaire.

# 2 LITERATURE REVIEW

2.1 THE USE OF MEDICINAL PLANTS FOR THERAPEUTIC PURPOSES: Some considerations

The use of plant species to treat and cure diseases is a practice that dates back to the dawn of civilization. Thus, from the moment man became aware that it was possible to modify the environment for his own benefit, he began to use certain plants for medicinal purposes.

It is important to note that this ancient practice has overcome all barriers and obstacles in its evolutionary process and has reached the present day, being widely used by a large part of the world's population as a therapeutic resource.

[a]Carriconde (2002) states that after World War II, medicine became very sophisticated and, with advances in health research, there was an increase in medicines produced from plants. And later, from synthetic compounds.

Thus, scientifically produced medicines on an industrial scale became more widespread and widely used, significantly reducing the use of medicinal plants as alternative cures.

However, the use of medicinal plants as a traditional practice still exists among peoples all over the world, and is more evident in developing countries, where most of the poor population does not have access to pharmaceutical medicines (CARRICONDE, 2002).

Even in industrialized countries such as the United States, around 25% of all prescription drugs dispensed by community pharmacies between 1959 and 1980 contained active substances from higher plants (MARTINS et al., 2000).

The World Health Organization (WHO), at its 3rd Assembly, recommended that member countries carry out research into the use of native flora for therapeutic purposes (FARNSWORTH; SOERJATO, 2005).

Associated with the diversity of plant species is also cultural diversity, which plays an important role in the case of medicinal plants. For it is from traditional knowledge, originating from different populations around the world, that countless medicines used today in Western medicine have been derived.

Scheffer; Ming and Araùjo (1998) note that widely used medicines such as emetine, vincristine, quinine, curare, diosgenin, pilocarpine, cocaine, among others, might not even be used in modern medicine if it weren't for the traditional use that local communities have made of these plants since ancient times.

A study by Martins et al. (2000) shows that of the more than 200,000 plant species that may exist in Brazil, at least half may have some therapeutic properties useful to the population. However, only 1% of these species have been the subject of adequate studies.

In view of this importance, research into these plants should receive the full support of public authorities. As well as the economic factor, the importance of national security and the preservation of the ecosystems in which these species are found should also be highlighted.

Pereira and Freitas (2008) report that basic and applied research into medicinal plants is being carried out in Paranà by the Klabim Agroforestry Company and the Caetano Munhoz da Rocha Foundation, in conjunction with the Federal University of Paranà, adding that the aim of this research is to produce new knowledge and effective medicines that are accepted by the population and health professionals.

According to Carriconde (2002), the future of medicine lies in medicinal herbs. Therapeutic nuclei no longer respond effectively to the needs of the market.

It should also be noted that this is compounded by the ineffectiveness of the chemical drugs currently used to treat cancer and other degenerative diseases, which shows the urgent need to look for new therapeutic nuclei. On the other hand, there is also a greater demand among consumers for less toxic natural products.

A study carried out by Agra and Silva (1993) showed that in the state of Paraiba the use of medicinal plants for therapeutic purposes is still quite common, especially in rural areas and also among low-income populations in urban areas. It is estimated that around 300 species are used for medicinal purposes throughout the state.

Ethnobotanical studies in this region will make a great contribution to recovering the knowledge and conceptualizations developed by the communities about the plant world, as well as the use made of these plants, with a view to improving the quality of life of the population.

2.2  THE USE OF MEDICINAL PLANTS: A historical approach

The use of medicinal plants as medicine is probably as old as man himself. Numerous stages have marked the evolution of the art of healing. However, it is difficult to demarcate them precisely, since medicine has long been associated with magical, mystical and ritualistic practices.

Whether they are considered spiritual beings or not, plants have acquired fundamental importance in folk medicine, due to their therapeutic or toxic properties, and are still widely used today (MARTINS et al., 2000).

According to Bragança (1998), the first detailed information on medicinal plants and their uses comes from China and dates back to the period between 2,500 and 3,000 BC, when the emperor Sheng-Nung used his body to feel the effects produced by various plants. In the end, that ruler wrote a treatise on the medicinal use of more than 300 species, called "Pen Tsao" or "The Book of Herbs".

It is important to note that the Egyptians, Assyrians and Hebrews had been cultivating various medicinal herbs since 2,300 BC. With these plants, they produced purgatives, vermifuges, diuretics, edibles and spices for cooking, as well as liquids and gums, which were used for embalming mummies (MARTINS et al., 2000).

In ancient Greece, plants and their therapeutic or toxic value were widely known. Hippocrates (460-377 B.C.), known as the "Father of Medicine", compiled a summary of the medical knowledge of his time in his work *Corpus Hippocratium,* indicating a plant remedy for each illness, as well as the appropriate treatment (MARTINS et al., 2000).

At the beginning of the Christian era, Dioscorides listed more than 500 drugs of plant origin in his treatise, "De Matèria Medica", describing the therapeutic use of each one (GUARIM NETO, 1996).

However, throughout the Middle Ages, medicine and the study of medicinal plants stagnated for a long time. The historical events that took place in Europe, such as the rise and fall of the Roman Empire and the strengthening of the Catholic Church, had an enormous influence on all the knowledge that existed at the time, including information about medicinal plants (BRAGANÇA, 1998).

From the 16th century onwards, during the great voyages, the flora of America and Africa was discovered as European dominions expanded. The missionaries in America learned from the natives how to use various plants for therapeutic purposes. The Aztecs, Mayans and Incas also contributed hallucinogenic, psychotropic and other plants used in healing and magical-religious rituals, such as coca (*Erythroxylum coca* Lamk.).

According to Bragança (1998), flora has been studied in Brazil since the time of colonization. The contribution of indigenous societies in passing on this knowledge is undeniable. Even before the discovery of Brazil, the Indians used annatto to paint and protect their bodies from insect bites, and various plants to cure diseases. And, believing in supernatural factors, the shamans associated plants with magic rituals and their treatments were passed down orally through the generations.

However, it should be emphasized that the use of plants in Brazil for the treatment of diseases has been greatly influenced by indigenous, African and European cultures (MARTINS et al. 2000).

The African influence is little known, but no less relevant. In the past, for black people, when someone fell ill it was because they were possessed by an evil spirit and a healer was responsible for expelling it through exorcism and the use of drugs, often of animal origin (RODRIGUES, 1998).

The European influence began in Brazil in 1579, with the arrival of the priests of the Society of Jesus, led by Father Manoel da Nóbrega. The Jesuits began to organize the so-called "Apothecaries of the Colleges", where they produced herbal medicines to treat illnesses. This initiative marks the beginning of hospital care in Brazil (BRAGANÇA, 1998).

Most of the medicinal herbs used in Brazil are of European origin. However, although they are not native, many of these plants reproduce spontaneously and form genotypes or varieties distinct from those that came with the Europeans during colonization (MARTINS et al., 2000).

Among the various medicinal species used in Brazil, the following stand out: colonia (*Alpinia speciosa* L.), lemon balm (*Lippia alba* Mill), big mint (*Plectrantus amboinicus* Lour.), man mint (*Plectrantus barbatus* Benth.), spearmint (*Mentha x villosa* Hudds.), *basil (Ocimum basilicum* L.), *pomegranate (Punica granatum L.),* rosemary (*Rosamarinus offinalis L.),* rue (*Ruta graveolens* L.) and ginger (*Zingiber officinale R.)* (CARRICONDE, 2002).

2.3 ETNOBOTANICS

The term Ethnobotany was first used by John William Harshberger in 1895 to refer to the study of the use of plants by the Aborigines. However, since ancient times, man has been concerned with analyzing and cataloguing the various uses of plants and the collection of information has contributed to scientific research (AMOROZO, 1996).

Jorge (2001) notes that the prefix "Ethno" indicates the way people look at the world. When used in connection with the name of a discipline, it indicates that researchers in these fields are looking for local perceptions within this academic approach.

For a long time, ethnobotanical research was known as a synonym for economic botany, and its history ran parallel to the evolution of systematic and economic botany. Explorers, traders, missionaries, anthropologists and botanists made observations about the use of plants by cultures other than Europeans, which appeared to be exotic, thus forming the roots of ethnobotany as an academic discipline (JORGE, 2001).

Initially, studies were only concerned with cataloging the uses of plants used by indigenous peoples around the world. Completing this thought, Prance (1995) recalls that it was with the work of Carolus Linnaeus that the history of botany and ethnobotany began. Linnaeus sent his students to different parts of the world, where they brought back a large number of new species, as well as data on the cultures they visited, the customs of the inhabitants and how they used the plants. The travel diaries of these students contained a wealth of ethnobotanical data that was analyzed and disseminated in the scientific world.

In 1886, Alphonse de Candolle published the book "Origin of cultivated plants", presenting an extensive study on the origin and distribution of plants cultivated for medicinal purposes (ALBUQUERQUE, 2002).

In 1887, Stephen Powers used the term "Botànica Aborigine" to describe the study of all forms of the plant world used by Aborigines. Subsequently, numerous works similar to this were carried out, which led to the first ethnobotanical studies with individual ethnic groups (JORGE, 2001).

According to Martins et al. (2000), ethnobotany is a part of ethnoecology that deals with plant relationships. Ethnoecology is the study that describes the interactions of local populations with the natural environment.

Ethnobotany is cited in the literature as one of the alternative paths that has evolved the most in recent years, thus making a significant contribution to the discovery of bioactive natural products (MACIEL; PINTO, VEIGA, 2002).

With the development of the natural sciences and, later, anthropology, the study of plants and their uses by different human groups took on a different perspective. It should be noted that from the mid-20th century onwards, the concept of ethnobotany evolved thanks to the contributions of various researchers (COTTON, 1996).

Today, this science not only looks at the use of plants, but also at the ways in which traditional communities manage them in order to obtain and maintain the resources they need.

Martin (1995) points out that ethnobotany studies:

a) the total interaction between traditional communities and the surrounding vegetation;

b)    all the plants used in a given crop.

c)    plant-human interrelationships, integrated into a dynamic ecosystem of natural and social components;

d)    the mutual relationships between plants and human cultures;

e)    how its exploitation by man influences its evolution;

f)    how plants are classified, named, used and managed;

Its meaning has been expanded by Jorge (2001), who suggests including research and evaluation of knowledge of all stages of the plant's life and the effects it has on the life history of peoples.

In 1967, Schultes broadened the concept of ethnobotany to include the relationship between man and the vegetation in his environment. In his research, Schultes incorporated botanical, anthropological, chemical and pharmaceutical data. He emphasized the importance of conserving ethnobotanical data, arguing that wars, increased commercial interests, tourism, among other factors, could lead to the disappearance of these cultures (PLOTKIN, 1995).

It is important to note that there are numerous definitions of the term "ethnobotany". Xolocotzi (2002) defined ethnobotany as the scientific field that studies the interactions between human beings and plants over time and in different environments.

Ford (2001), in turn, defined it as the study of the direct interrelationships between humans and plants. However, Ming and Amaral Júnior (2005) broadened this concept to include all aspects of the human relationship with plants, whether concrete (material use, conservation, cultural use, disuse) or open (cult symbols, folklore, taboos, sacred plants). However, because of this scope, the practice of ethnobotany requires interdisciplinary elaboration and collaboration. Prance (1995) emphasizes that the participation of researchers from the fields of Agronomy, Anthropology, Botany, Ecology, Forestry Engineering and Chemistry has enabled significant progress in ethnobotanical research, based on the principle that a multiple approach has been taken to how man perceives, classifies and uses plants.

According to Alexiades (1996), ethnobotany represents the study of human societies, past and present, and all types of interrelationships within them, be they ecological, evolutionary or symbolic.

More objectively, Jorge and Morais (2003) analyze ethnobotany through the relationship between human beings and plant resources, seeking to answer the following questions:

a)   which plants are available in a given environment;

b)   which plants are recognized as resources;

c)   how ethnobotanical knowledge is distributed among the population;

d)   how individuals perceive, differentiate and classify vegetation and how it is used and managed.

Based on the definitions presented by various studies on ethnobiology produced in the United States, Amorozo (1996) defines ethnobotany as the discipline that deals with the study of the knowledge and conceptualizations developed by any society about the plant world, encompassing both the way in which a social group classifies plants and how they use them. A qualitative and chronological analysis of the work carried out shows that there has been a conceptual and methodological evolution in ethnobotany. Currently, quantitative ethnobotany is becoming part of the approach, as a complement to the studies.

Currently, on the basis of work already carried out, ethnobotany can be understood as the study of the interrelationships (material or symbolic) between human beings and plants, to which must be added environmental and cultural factors, as well as the local concepts that are developed in relation to plants and the use that is made of them (JORGE; MORAIS, 2003).

In Brazil, for example, the Germans J. B. von Spix and Carl von Martius, in the 19th century, made notes on the use of plants by the indigenous people. Much earlier (in the 17th century) in the north-east of Brazil, the Dutch Guilherme Piso and Georg Marggraf collected plants and recorded uses known to the indigenous people (ALBUQUERQUE, 2002).

The vast majority of ethnobotanical work in Brazil has been carried out with indigenous tribes, mainly in the Amazon, and has dealt with the uses that the Indians made of plants, surveying and recording the forms of use given by the historical relationship of these communities with the rainforest (AMOROZO, 1996).

In the Northeast, little research has been carried out with communities, with Sales and Lima (1995) carrying out a survey of plants used for various purposes in the micro-region of Soledade, Paraiba, in areas of caatinga. In this study, the species were identified according to the ways in which they were used, the main ones being medicinal (88%), fuel

(80%) and food (35%). The percentage of use of the species cited was also calculated, with the 'catingueira' (*Caesalpinia pyramidalis*) standing out with 95% for various forms of use.

On the other hand, Silva (2001) carried out ethnobotanical studies in communities located in the Litoral-Mata area of the state of Pernambuco, identifying the medicinal plants used and tracing the socio-economic profile of their users. In this study, 54 unstructured interviews were conducted to find out which plants were useful to these localities, classifying them in the categories of food, commerce, construction, medicinal, technological and other uses. A total of 392 native and cultivated species were recorded.

Albuquerque and Andrade (2002) studied botanical and traditional knowledge in a rural community located in the municipality of Alagoinha, in the agreste region of the state of Pernambuco. A variety of research methods were used, including floristic surveys in agroforestry systems and natural vegetation. The people identified and/or use more than 180 plant species distributed into 10 categories: food, medicinal, wood (for fuel, construction, etc.), domestic use (technology), fodder, poison, insect repellent, ornamentation, shade and mystical.

However, due to its biodiversity, Brazil is considered a rich country in terms of medicinal plants, even in the northeast region, where the Caatinga biome predominates, which despite its limitations, has several species that are used in both ethnobotany and ethnoveterinary.

2.4 ETHNOVETERINARY

There are many concepts put forward for the term "Ethnoveterinary". In a broad sense, Ethnoveterinary can be conceptualized as the science that preserves and values the knowledge of popular practices used to treat and prevent diseases that affect animals.

In a more technical definition, Càrceres et al. (2004) point out that Ethnoveterinary can be conceptualized as the science that studies and values traditional beliefs, knowledge, techniques, methods and practices, which are used in the process of promoting animal health, adding that the use of ethnoveterinary practices is justified due to the following factors:

a)    high costs for veterinary services;

b)    growing demand for organic food, especially in terms of the use of herbal medicine;

c)    difficulty in acquiring synthetic drugs;

Ethnoveterinary is used in all regions of the world. Like ethnobotany, it is also used for thousands of years. Farmers all over the world use popular practices and knowledge to prevent and treat diseases that commonly appear in their livestock and pets (MONTEIRO, 2010).

It is important to emphasize that Ethnoveterinary can be seen as the systematic investigation and practical application of popular knowledge in the promotion of animal health care (ANDRADE et al., 2012).

Today, several countries around the world make extensive use of ethnoveterinary medicine. Among these are Canada and Italy, where popular knowledge related to treating animals with medicinal plants has been used and passed on for centuries, contributing significantly to maintaining animal health and productivity (MONTEIRO, 2010).

Thanks to the incentives given to Ethnobotany by the World Health Organization, Ethnoveterinary has also been receiving attention from many researchers, based on the principle that this science combines the advantages of Traditional Medicine (TM) with the Modern Medical System (MMS), as highlighted by Maciel; Pinto; Veiga (2006).

In the specific case of Brazil, ethnoveterinary medicine is widely used in all its regions. Particularly in the Northeast, it is presented as an alternative that has helped to solve many of the problems faced by small, medium and large farmers with regard to animal health, based on the principle that it is practically cost-free and highly effective, especially when used to control gastrointestinal diseases (MONTEIRO, 2010).

# 3  MATERIAL AND METHODS

## 3.1  TYPE OF STUDY

The study was carried out using a descriptive field study with a qualitative approach.

## 3.2  CHARACTERIZATION OF THE STUDY AREA

The study was carried out in the 14$^a$ Administrative Region of EMATER-PB, made up of the municipalities of Cajazeirinhas, Condado, Coremas, Lagoa, Paulista, Pombal, Sao Bentinho, Sao Domingos and Vista Serrana, with the city of Pombal as its headquarters, which stands out in the Paraíba sertao as one of the regional hubs, along with Patos, Souza and Cajazeiras.

**Figure 1. Administrative Regions of EMATER-PB**

In this region, the predominant vegetation is the Caatinga, made up of xerophytic plants, which lose their foliage during the dry periods and regrow at the beginning of the first rains.

The municipalities that make up this Administrative Region are located in the so-called 'Poligono das Secas' (Drought Polygon) and, for this reason, in climatological terms, it has a hot and dry semi-arid climate, according to the Koppen classification. Temperatures are high during the day, easing at night, with annual variations within a range of 23 to 30° C, with occasional higher peaks, mainly during the dry season (MASCARENHAS et al., 2005).

Rainfall is not only low, but also irregular, with annual averages of 1,105 mm/year. Due to fluctuations in climatic factors, there can be variations up or down the range. In general, it is characterized by the presence of only two seasons: the dry season, which is the summer, with a climax from September to December, and the rainy season, called winter by the sertanejo.

The region where this study was carried out has a relief that is included in the so-called 'Planicie Sertaneja', which is an extensive flattened pediplano where, locally, elongated residual elevations stand out and are aligned with the trend of the regional geological structure (CARVALHO; TRAVASSOS; MACIEL, 2002).

In hydrographic terms, the municipalities that make up the $14^a$ Administrative Region of EMATER-PB belong to the Piranhas River basin, being part of the Piancó River sub-basin, with an intermittent flow regime.

The main water reservoir in this region is the Coremas-Mae D'àgua Dam, considered the largest in the state of Paraiba, with a capacity of 1,358,000,000 $m^3$ of water.

Access to the municipalities that make up EMATER-PB's 14th Administrative Region from Joao Pessoa is via the BR-230 highway to the city of Pombal, initially passing through Condado and Sao Bentinho. From Pombal, it goes to Cajazeirinhas and Coremas, following the PB-426. Access to Lagoa from Pombal is via the PB-325.

Access to Paulista is via the BR-427 and then the PB-293. From Pombal to Sao Domingos, access is via the PB-338, while to Vista Serrana, part of the access is via the BR-427, followed by a side road that runs for 9 km.

3.3  POPULATION AND SAMPLE

The survey informants were the heads of household, both men and women. Initially, 30 people were interviewed in rural areas and in the headquarters of each municipality, i.e. in the nine municipalities listed above, thus totaling 270 participants. Of these 270 participants, five (05) people per municipality were selected by lot, so that the sample to be analyzed was reduced to 45 participants.

3.4  DATA COLLECTION INSTRUMENT

A previously structured questionnaire containing objective and subjective questions was used as an instrument for data collection, with the aim of achieving the objectives set for this research, which concerns the use of medicinal plants for the treatment of diseases in humans and animals, as well as the association of these plants with bee honey for the treatment of diseases in humans.

The questionnaire consisted of two parts. The first was designed to collect the data needed to draw up a profile of the sample interviewed. The second part contained questions related to the objectives of the research, with the aim of collecting data on the sample:

a)    The use of medicinal plants to treat diseases in humans and animals;

b)    Identification of the plant used;

c)    Identification of the disease/illness being treated;

d)    The treatment period in humans and animals;

e)    The plant used is actually grown or harvested;

f)    Identifying the part of the plant used to prepare the home remedy for the desired treatment;

g)    The fact that he learned to use plants for medicinal purposes;

1)    The existence of contraindications in humans and animals;

h)    The type of bee that produces the honey used in the process of association with medicinal plants.

3.5 DATA COLLECTION

Data was collected in two stages between March and June 2014. In the first, the initial 270 participants were interviewed. After the draw, we returned to the municipalities that make up the 14$^a$ Administrative Region of EMATER-PB, where we visited all 45 (forty-five) people drawn at home.

During the interviews, we tried to avoid the direct influence of other people. To this end, individual interviews were carried out at different times, even when two or more people lived in the same place.

3.6 ANALYSIS OF THE DATA COLLECTED

Once collected, the data was analyzed quantitatively using the descriptive model and presented in the form of graphs and tables. The discussion of the results was supported by the relevant literature.

# 4   RESULTS AND DISCUSSION

## 3.7 PROFILE OF THE SAMPLE INTERVIEWED

The first step was to outline the profile of the sample interviewed in this survey. The data relating to gender, age group and occupation are shown in Table 1.

Table 1. Profile of the sample interviewed in the 14[a] Administrative Region of EMATER-PB, based in Pombal

| VARIABLES | QUANTITY | PERCENTAGE |
|---|---|---|
| **Sex** | | |
| Male | 27 | 60,00% |
| Female | 18 | 40,00% |
| **TOTAL** | **45** | **100,00%** |
| **Age range** | | |
| Between 31-40 years old | 3 | 6,66% |
| Between 41-50 years old | 8 | 17,76% |
| Between 51-60 years old | 11 | 24,42% |
| Between 61-70 years old | 14 | 31,08% |
| Between 71-80 years old | 7 | 15,54% |
| Between 81-90 years old | 2 | 4,54% |
| **TOTAL** | **45** | **100,00%** |
| **Profession** | | |
| Farmer | 36 | 79,92% |
| Merchant | 1 | 2,22% |
| Teacher | 3 | 6,66% |
| Housewife | 5 | 11,20% |
| **TOTAL** | **45** | **100,00%** |

Analyzing the data collected and presented in Table 1, it can be seen that of the 45 participants in this survey, 60% were male and 40% female. 27 men and 18 women were interviewed in the municipalities that make up the 14th Administrative Region of Emater-

PB (Cajazeirinhas, Condado, Coremas, Lagoa, Paulista, Pombal, Sao Betinho, Sao Domingos and Vista Serrana), based in the city of Pombal.

Marinho; Silva and Andrade (2011), carrying out an ethnobotanical survey of medicinal plants in a caatinga area in the municipality of Sao José de Espinharas, Paraiba state, interviewed a sample made up of men and women in percentages equal to 50%, a fact that differs very little from the profile of the sample interviewed in this study.

With regard to the age of the interviewees, the data collected shows that the majority of participants were aged between 60 and 69 (31.08%), followed by those aged between 50 and 59 (24.42%). The age group with the lowest number of participants was between 80 and 89 (n = 2), representing 4.54% of the sample interviewed. As for the other data, 6.66% of those interviewed said they were aged between 30 and 39, and 17.76% said they were aged between 40 and 49.

Evaluating the use of bee honey associated with medicinal plants in the Vàrzea Comprida dos Oliveira community, in the municipality of Pombal-PB, Andrade et al. (2012) interviewed a sample made up of participants aged between 31-40 years (35%), 41-50 years (22.5%), 61-70 years (15%), 51-60 years (12.5%), 71-78 years (10%) and 27-30 years (5%), respectively, results very different from the profile presented by the sample interviewed in this study.

The data collected and presented in Table 1 also shows that 79.92% of the 45 interviewees in the nine municipalities mentioned above were farmers (n = 36) and 11.20% were housewives; 2.22% said they were traders (n = 1) and 6.66% said they were teachers (n = 3).

A sample interviewed by Guerra et al. (2010), in the rural community of Moacir Lucena, in the municipality of Apodi-RN, was made up mostly of 75% farmers, a profile that is somewhat similar to that of the sample considered in this study.

3.8 DATA RELATED TO THE RESEARCH OBJECTIVES

Initially, the participants in this survey were asked if they used medicinal plants to treat any illnesses, both in humans and in animals. The data collected in this questionnaire is shown in Graph 1.

**Graph 1 - Distribution of the sample as to whether they use any type of medicinal plant**

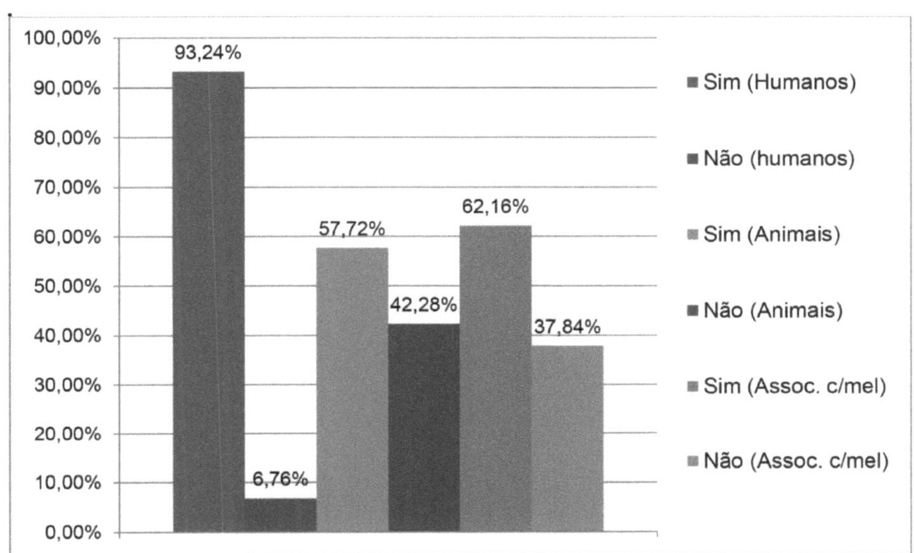



Analyzing the data collected in the nine municipalities together, it can be seen that 93.24% of those interviewed use medicinal plants to treat diseases in humans and that 62.16% usually associate the medicinal plant with bee honey. With regard to the use of medicinal plants in the treatment of diseases affecting animals, 57.72% said that they usually used this form of treatment.

With regard to ethnobotany, a similar result was found by Teixeira and Melo (2006) when they carried out a survey in the Pajeù sertao, in Pernambuco, where they found that 100% of those interviewed used medicinal plants in cases of illness.

In the process of associating medicinal plants with bee honey, Melo Filho (2014) showed that in the municipality of Catolé do Rocha-PB, this association was attested to by 79.17% of the interviewees, while in the present study, the percentage recorded was 62.16%, slightly lower.

Another study, whose results are very close to those found in this study, was carried out by Andrade et al. (2012), revealing that 50% of the farmers they interviewed in the municipality of Pombal-PB used medicinal plants to treat diseases affecting their animals.

Taking into account the fact that the use of medicinal plants is widespread among the participants, both in the treatment of diseases in humans and in animals, we were concerned to identify in this sample the main plant species used in each segment. Graph 2 shows the plant species most commonly used by participants to treat diseases in humans.

This chart lists the medicinal plants by number of mentions by the interviewees.

**Graph 2 - Distribution of the sample regarding the main medicinal plants used to treat diseases in humans**

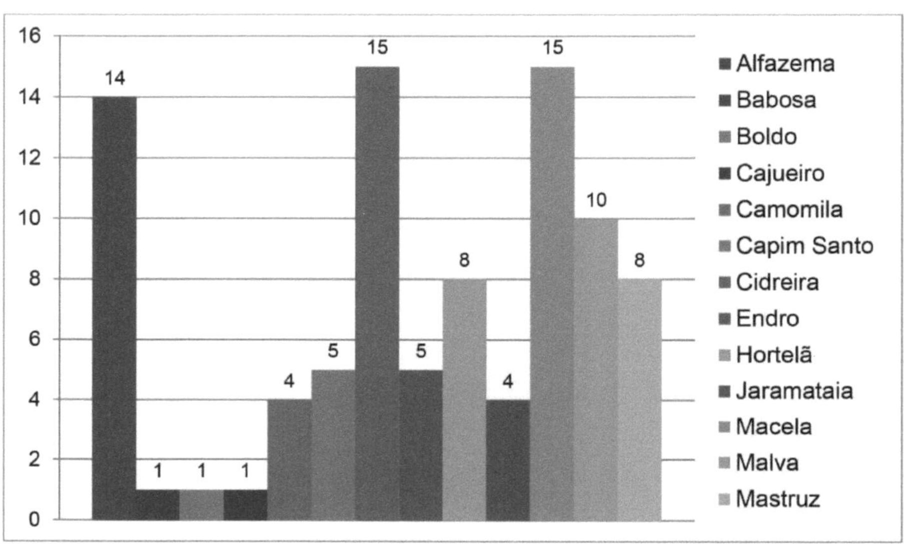


Analysis of the data presented in Graph 2 shows that the sample interviewed uses the following medicinal plants to treat human illnesses: lavender (*Lavandula spica* Cav.), *aloe vera* L.), boldo (*Peumus boldus),* cashew (*Anacardium occidentale L.),* capim santo (*Cymbopogon citratus* (DC) Stapf.), lemon balm (*Lippia alba (Mill.) N. E. Brown. Brown.*), chamomile (*Matricària recutita),* dill (*Anethum graveolens),* mint (*Mentha sp.),* jaramataia (*Vitex gardneriana),* macela (*Egletes viscosa* (L.) Less.), mallow (*Malva parviflora L.)* and mastruz (*Chenopodium ambrosoides* L.).

However, among these, the most commonly used are: lemon balm, macela, lavender, holy grass, mastruz and mint.

Guerra et al. (2010) in a study carried out in the Moacir Lucena Settlement, in the municipality of Apodi-RN, revealed that the species most cited by the interviewees were *Anacardium Occidentale* L. (cashew), *Chenopodium ambrosoides* L. (mastruz), Anacardiaceae (aroeira) and *Ocimum basilicum* L (manjericâo). These data are very different from those obtained in the present study, which also mentions cashew trees and mastruz.

However, in a more recent study carried out in the municipality of Catolé do Rocha [60 km from Pombal, the main focus of this research], Melo Filho (2014) determined that the medicinal plants most used in that region were, by number of mentions, mallow, mint, rosemary and lemon balm, respectively.

In another study, Pontes et al. (2012) pointed out that medicinal plants are commonly used in the Northeast of Brazil to prepare home remedies to treat human illnesses, with the following species standing out: mint; pomegranate; melão de São Caetano capim santo and lemon balm.

A more comprehensive study by Lima et al. (2006) lists fifty species of plants that can be used to combat various diseases that affect human beings. This study also describes the different ways of preparing the plants identified.

Among the medicinal plants surveyed in this study and described by Lima et al. (2006), the following stand out: babosa, cashew, capim santo, erva cidreira, hortelâ, macela and mastruz.

Once we had identified the main medicinal plants used by the participants in this study, we tried to determine in which situations these plant species were used.

Table 1 shows the medicinal plants used to treat diseases that affect humans, and their respective uses.

**Table 1 - Medicinal plants mentioned by the interviewees and their respective uses in the treatment of humans**

| Medicinal plant | Use |
| --- | --- |
| Lavender | Bronchitis, intestinal problems, constipation, gastritis, amoebae |
| Babosa | Healing, prostate, cancer, anti-inflammatory |
| Bilberry | Liver, intestinal problems |
| Cashew | Anti-inflammatory, gastritis, healing |
| Chamomile | Soothing |
| Holy grass | Soothing, fever, headache |
| Cidreira | Intestinal problems, calming, fever, opening the appetite, |
| Dill | Blood pressure, indigestion, pain |
| Mint | Flu, sinusitis, headache |

| Jaramataia | Prostate, anti-inflammatory |
| --- | --- |
| Macela | Intestinal problems, indigestion, amoeba, constipation |
| Mallow | Gastric ulcer, expectorant, anti-inflammatory |
| Mastruz | Ulcer, healing, gastritis, flu |

An analysis of Table 1 shows that lavender, aloe vera, macela and mastruz are the plant species used by the participants in this research for the greatest number of diseases affecting human beings.

Among the most widely used medicinal plants, lavender, mint and mastruz are widely used to fight colds and bronchitis. In the specific case of mastruz, when combined with milk, it is used to combat gastritis and intestinal ulcers, as is lavender when used in tea or cooked form.

A study carried out by Melo Filho (2014) also revealed that mallow, mint, rosemary and lemon balm are widely used plants in the municipality of Catolé do Rocha-PB to treat colds, fevers, migraines and colic, results that are in line with those found in this study.

On the other hand, in a more detailed study, Morais (2011) recorded that lavender, in addition to the ailments listed in Table 1, can also be used to combat rheumatism, neuralgia, nervous excitement, asthma, etc.; while lemon balm is used as a rejuvenator, revitalizer, antidepressant, antiallergic, carminative, hypotensive and antispasmodic.

Morais (2011) adds that as well as fighting liver and stomach ailments, boldo can also be used to treat hepatitis, insomnia and diabetes. And mallow can be used to fight flu, pneumonia and colds.

With regard to macela, the sample interviewed uses this plant to treat a range of intestinal diseases, including indigestion and constipation. This plant is also used to combat some parasitic diseases, such as amoeba.

Haerffner et al. (2012) state that macela is used to combat headaches, sore throats, stomach aches, intestinal colic and digestion.

As for capim santo, this research has shown that it is used as a calming agent and to combat fevers and headaches.

According to Lima et al. (2006) the tea made from its leaves is tasty and aromatic and can also be used to relieve uterine cramps, as well as to treat nervousness.

The data presented in Table 1 also shows that in addition to being used to treat a range of intestinal problems, lemon balm is also indicated as a tranquilizer and to combat fevers, as well as serving to "open up" the appetite.

Corroborating the data collected in the present study, Lima et al. (2006) show that lemon balm can be used as a calming and spasmolytic agent, as well as for treating uterine and intestinal cramps.

The data in Table 1 also shows that aloe is a medicinal plant that not only reduces the risk of inflammation, but also acts as a healing agent and, according to the interviewees, has a great effect on fighting cancer, especially prostate cancer.

The use of aloe in the treatment of cancer has been mentioned by several authors, including Morais (2011) and Vestena et al. (2010). However, the latter authors took a more detailed approach, stating that aloe has the ability to reduce intestinal cancer, as well as having a healing, antibacterial and antifungal action.

After identifying the main medicinal plants used to treat diseases that affect humans, the same concern was expressed in relation to animals. The species mentioned by the interviewees are shown in Graph 3.

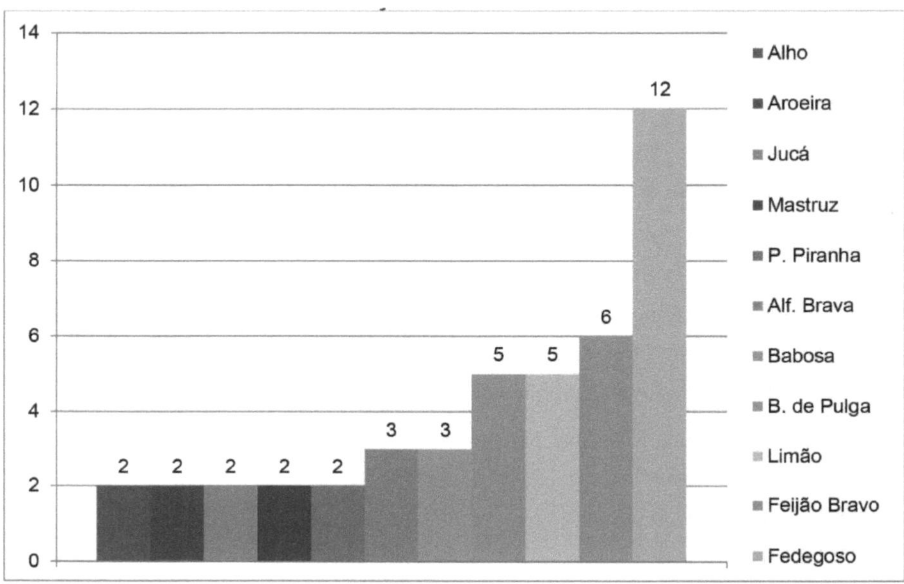


The data presented in Graph 3 shows that the interviewees commonly use garlic (*Allium sativum*), mastic (*Myracrodruon urundeuva* All.), jucà (*Caesalpinia ferrea Martius*), mastruz (*Chenopodium ambrosoides* L.), pau piranha (*Guapira graciliflora*), lavender (*Lavandula spica* Cav.), *aloe vera (Aloe vera* L.), flea potato (*Operculina macrocarpa* [Linn] Urb.), lemon, wild bean and fedegoso (*Senna occidentals* L.) as medicinal plants in the treatment of diseases affecting their animals, with the following species standing out: flea potato, lemon, wild bean and fedegoso.

In contrast to the results found in this study, Silva et al. (2005) show that holy grass (*Cymbopogon citratus*) can be used to treat gastrointestinal nematodes in sheep. And that the species mastruz (*Chenopodium ambrosioides*) can also be used to combat the same disease.

Oliveira et al. (2009) point out that aroeira is used to combat pain. However, the risk of its use can lead to abortion, especially in cows and sheep.

Secondly, we tried to determine in which situations these plant species were used. Table 2 lists the clinical veterinary complications that lead to the use of the plant species most cited by the interviewees in the nine municipalities surveyed.

**Table 2 - Medicinal plants mentioned by the interviewees and their respective uses in treating animals**

| Medicinal plant | Use |
| --- | --- |
| Garlic | Chicken game |
| Mastic | Scabies |
| Jucà | Healing, anti-inflammatory |
| Mastruz | Fighting worms |
| Piranha stick | Vacuuming (expelling the placenta) |
| Wild Lavender | Fever |
| Babosa | Healing, fever, sadness. |
| Flea potatoes | Fighting worms and diarrhea |
| Lemon | Chicken game |
| Bravo Beans | To vacate (expel the placenta), mal triste. |
| Fedegoso | Vacuuming (expelling the placenta) |

Based on Table 2, it can be seen that in the opinion of the interviewees, the flea potato is used to combat worms and diarrhea in animals. As for lemon, it is widely used to combat a disease popularly known in the north-east of Brazil as "gogo" among chickens, which translates into a kind of bird flu.

According to the data presented in Table 2, it can be seen that wild beans and fedegoso, the two most frequently mentioned species, are used mainly as post-partum medication in cattle, with the aim of expelling the remains of the placenta, an act that is commonly known in the interior of Paraiba by the expression "desocupar", cleaning the cow's uterus after calving.

A study carried out by Sousa (2012) reveals that aroeira has a wide application in ethnoveterinary medicine, being used to treat general inflammations and to "clear up" the calving of cattle.

Dantas et al. (2009) also reported the use of medicinal plants to treat anemia, snakebite, yaws, flu, infectious coryza and vomiting, medical indications reported less frequently in this study.

In a third step, we tried to determine which species of medicinal plants are used to treat diseases that affect humans, in association with bee honey. The answers given by the interviewees to this question were transformed into data and presented in Graph 4.

**Graph 4 - Distribution of the sample in terms of the main medicinal plants used to treat diseases in humans, in combination with bee honey**

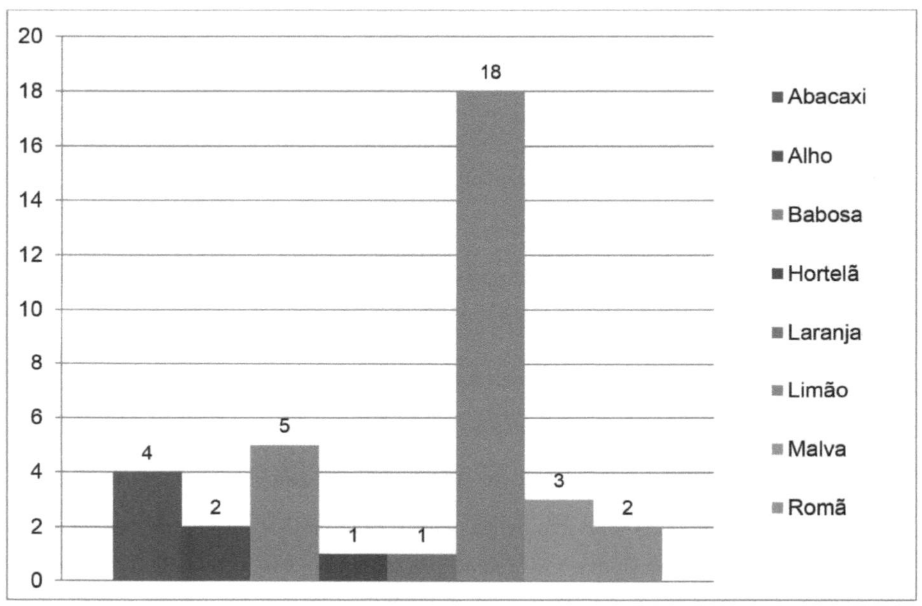


Graph 4 shows that, according to the interviewees, the plant species that are commonly used in combination with bee honey are

the fight against diseases that affect humans, are the following: pineapple, garlic, aloe, mint (*Mentha sp.*), orange (*Citrus sinensis L.*), lemon (*Citrus spp.*), mallow and pomegranate, among which the following stand out: lemon, aloe and pineapple.

More or less similar results were found by Andrade (2012), in a study carried out in Pombal-PB, showing that this association is more frequent in that municipality involving lemon, orange, mint, pomegranate and acerola, as well as garlic, the latter in small quantities.

Subsequently, it was determined in which situations medicinal plants associated with bee honey are used to treat diseases in humans. The data collected is shown in Table 3.

**Table 3 - Medicinal plants associated with bee honey, mentioned by the interviewees and their respective uses in the treatment of human diseases**

| Medicinal plant | Use |
| --- | --- |
| Pineapple | Flu |
| Garlic | Expectorant, cough |
| Babosa | Gastritis, Anti-inflammatory, healing, cancer |
| Mint | Flu, cough |
| Orange | Flu, cough |
| Lemon | Flu, cough, bronchitis |
| Mallow | Flu, cough |
| Româ | Anti-inflammatory |

Table 3 shows that most of the medicinal plants associated with bee honey mentioned by the interviewees are used to combat colds and coughs, as well as bronchitis, and garlic also has the characteristic of being an expectorant.

Aloe vera, like pomegranate, also has anti-inflammatory properties. However, according to the interviewees, this species combined with bee honey is used as a healing and anti-inflammatory agent, and is also used to fight different types of cancer.

Andrade et al. (2012), studying the use of bee honey associated with medicinal plants in the community of Vàrzea Comprida dos Oliveiras, in the municipality of Pombal-PB, showed that the use of bee honey associated with medicinal plants is more directed towards curing respiratory tract disorders, especially colds and flu.

The fourth question sought to determine whether the use of medicinal plants cures diseases in humans and animals. The data collected is shown in Graph 5.

**Graph 5 - Distribution of the sample as to whether they had ever treated someone or an animal with medicinal plants and managed to obtain a cure**

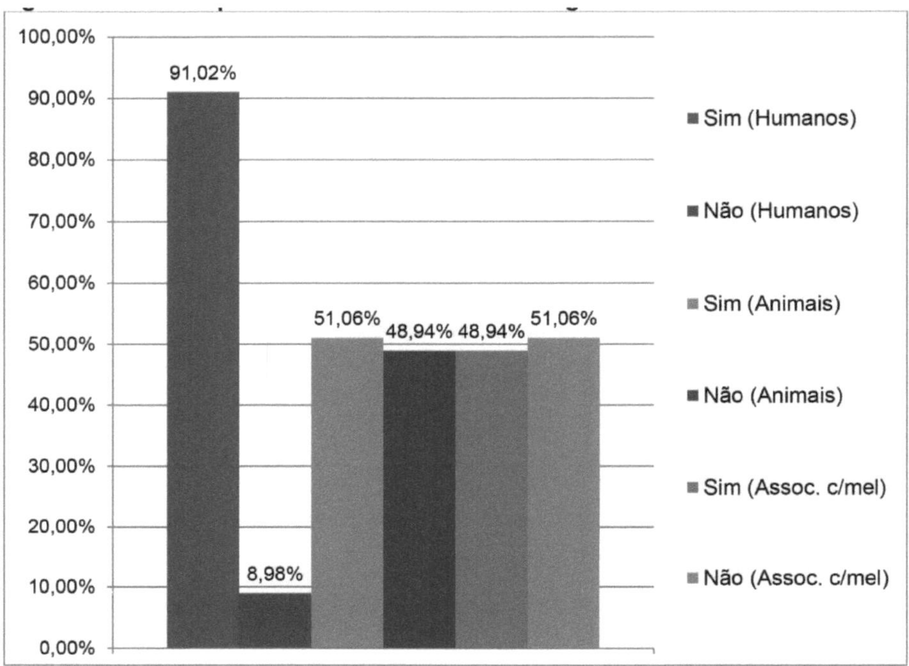


An analysis of the data presented in Graph 5 shows that when medicinal plants are used to treat diseases in humans, they achieve a greater number of cures. This was attested to by 91.02% of the participants interviewed. When used on animals, however, the healing power is lower, and was only attested to by 51.06% of the participants, which represents just over half of the sample.

When it came to treating the illnesses mentioned in Table 3, only 48.94% of the interviewees attested to being cured by using medicinal plants combined with honey.

The fifth question asked the interviewees how long they had been treated in the three situations, i.e. when medicinal plants were used to treat diseases in humans, in animals and when they were used in combination with bee honey. Graph 6 shows the results of this question.

**Graph 6 - Distribution of the sample regarding the duration of treatment using some type of medicinal plant**

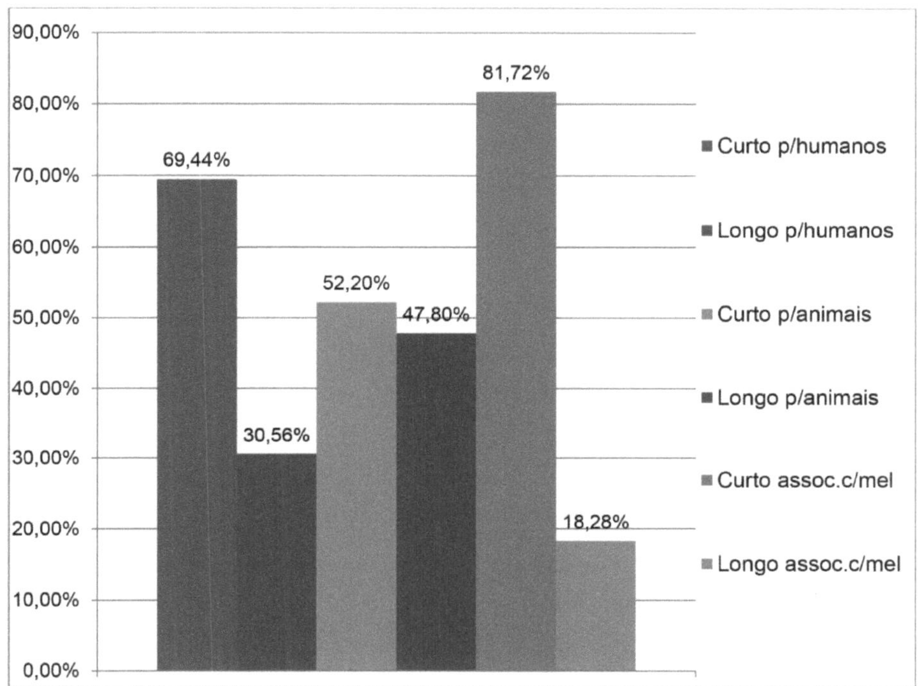


According to the data shown in Graph 6, treatment is shorter in cases where the medicinal plant is combined with bee honey and this was attested to by 81.72% of the participants, who initially stated that they used medicinal plants to combat illnesses that affect human beings.

When the medicinal plant alone was used to combat human ailments, the short treatment period was attested to by 69.44% of the participants.

As for the period of treatment for the animals, this was attested to as short by 52.20% of the participants who declared that they used medicinal plants to combat the illnesses affecting their herds.

Addressing the use of medicinal plants in the treatment of diseases that affect humans, Lacerda et al. (2013) showed that according to 94% of those interviewed in a rural community in the Paraíba municipality of Pombal, the treatment period is short.

These results are in line with those presented in this study, when the medicinal plant was combined with bee honey. They were much higher when only the medicinal plant was used (69.44%).

However, results similar to those found in this study were revealed by Araùjo (2011) in the municipality of Pombal, more specifically in the Jacu community, where the majority of people interviewed (67%) said that they were cured in a short period of time when they used herbal medicine to treat their illnesses.

As for the use of medicinal plants to treat animals, the results found in this study differ from those revealed by Teixeira and Melo (2006) in a study carried out in the interior of the state of Pernambuco, which showed that the time taken to obtain a cure through ethnoveterinary medicine is long, according to 62% of the interviewees.

This study showed that this time is short, according to the information provided by 52.22% of the participants, who live in the municipalities of Cajazeirinhas, Condado, Coremas, Lagoa, Pombal, Paulista, Sâo Bentinho, Sâo Domingos and Vista Serrana.

The sixth question asked the interviewees whether they grew any medicinal plants on their properties. Graph 7 shows the data collected from this question.

**Graph 7 - Distribution of the sample as to whether they grow any species of medicinal plant on their properties**

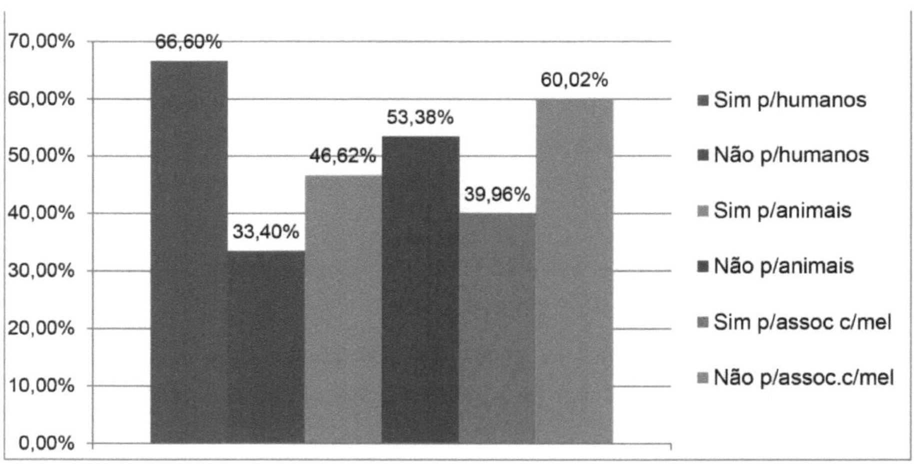


Based on the data presented in Graph 7, it can be seen that 66.60% of the interviewees grow some kind of medicinal plant on their property [or in their backyard] to treat human illnesses; 46.62% grow these species to treat animal illnesses. And 39.96% grow species which, together with bee honey, are used to treat diseases in humans.

The data presented in this research concerns the municipalities of Pombal, Condado, Sao Bentinho, Cajazeirinhas, Coremas, Paulista, Vista Serrana, Lagoa and Sao Domingos, which in turn make up the so-called 14ª Administrative Region of EMATER-PB, based in the municipality of Pombal.

In a study carried out only in the municipality of Pombal, Andrade (2012) showed that 58.82% of those interviewed did not cultivate the plants they consumed as herbal products, which is the opposite of the situation revealed in this study, since 66.60% of those interviewed cultivate the species used to treat diseases in humans.

However, this percentage was lower than that found by Melo Filho (2014) in a survey carried out in Catolé do Rocha, also in the Paraíba sertao, which showed that 81.66% of those interviewed cultivated the medicinal plant species they consumed. These results are higher than those found in this study.

Marinho; Silva and Andrade (2011) show that in Sâo José de Espinharas, PB, the population has free access to medicinal plants, as 54% of those interviewed obtain the plants for consumption directly from the forest or grow them in their own homes.

The seventh question asked participants which part of the medicinal plant they commonly use to treat diseases in humans and animals. The data collected is shown in Graph 8.

Specifically, in this case, we took into account not the number of participants, but the plant species cited for the treatment of diseases in humans and animals, as well as those that are frequently associated with bee honey, shown in Graphs 2, 3 and 4.

**Graph 8 - Distribution of the sample regarding the parts of plants used to treat diseases in animals and humans (associated with honey or not)**

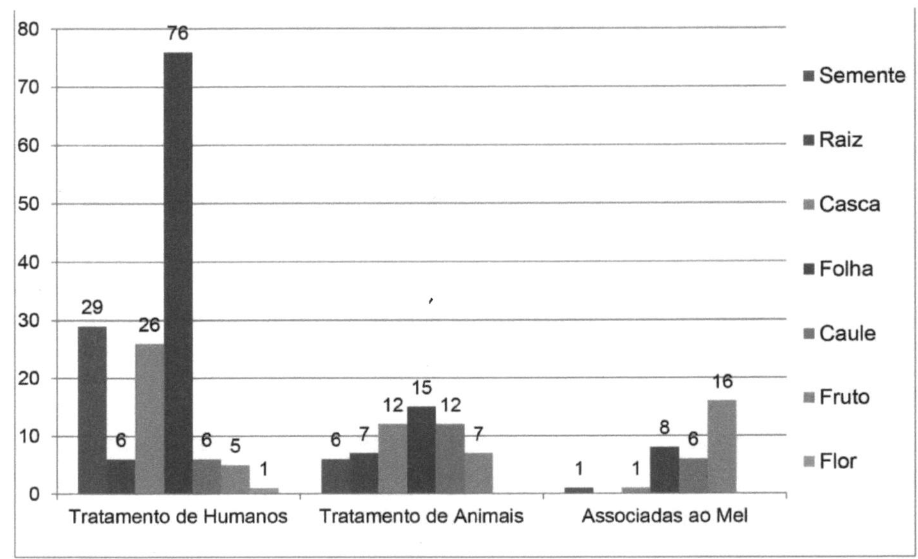



When analyzing the data presented in Graph 8, it can be seen that the leaves are the part of medicinal plants most used to treat diseases that affect humans, followed by seeds and bark.

Corroborating the data revealed in this study, Santos; Lolis and Belo (2006) showed that the parts of the plants most used in the preparation of herbal medicines are the leaves and the bark, with infusion, decoction and tincture being the methods of preparation.

A study carried out by Mosca and Loiola (2009) showed that among farmers in Rio Grande do Norte, the most commonly used parts of medicinal plants are the leaves, followed by the fruit and roots, seeds and flowers, bark, latex, bulb and stem, when used to treat human ailments.

Similar results to those obtained in this study were found in the surveys carried out by Amorozo (2002) and Teixeira and Melo (2006), who cited the leaves as the plant parts most used by the population.

However, a study carried out by Albuquerque and Andrade (2002) in Alagoinha, Pernambuco, shows that the bark was the most commonly used part in that municipality to produce homemade medicines to treat animal diseases.

Marinho; Silva and Andrade (2011) show that the parts of the plant most used in the preparation of home remedies are the root, stem bark, leaf, flower, fruit and seed. And although the leaves and roots are widely used in the preparation of home remedies, the stem bark is most commonly used in the form of decoctions and infusions for internal use.

With regard to the treatment of illnesses that affect animals, this research showed that the part of the medicinal plant that is most used is the leaf, followed by the bark and the stem. There is also good use of the fruit and root. Although they detected the use of leaves, stems and fruit in the preparation of home remedies for the treatment of animals, Andrade et al. (2012) did not find them in the same order [as presented in this study]. In the study carried out by those researchers in the municipality of Pombal-PB, the following order of use was obtained: stem, fruit and leaf.

Evaluating the use of medicinal plants in the rural community of Moacir Lucena, in the municipality of Apodi-RN, Guerra et al. (2010) found that the parts of the plants most commonly used to prepare medicines were leaves and bark, as well as fruit, flowers and seeds, results which are consistent with those revealed by this study.

As for the medicinal plants that are associated with bee honey, according to the interviewees, the most used part is the fruit, followed by the leaf and the stem. Subsequently, an attempt was made to determine the state of use of the plant for medicinal purposes. The data collected was condensed and presented in Graph 9, for the three situations proposed, i.e. human use, animal use and associated with bee honey for human use.

In this case, the number of participants interviewed was not taken into account, but rather the number of plant species mentioned that have medicinal uses.

**Graph 9 - Distribution of the sample regarding the status of plants used to treat diseases in animals and humans (associated with honey or not)**

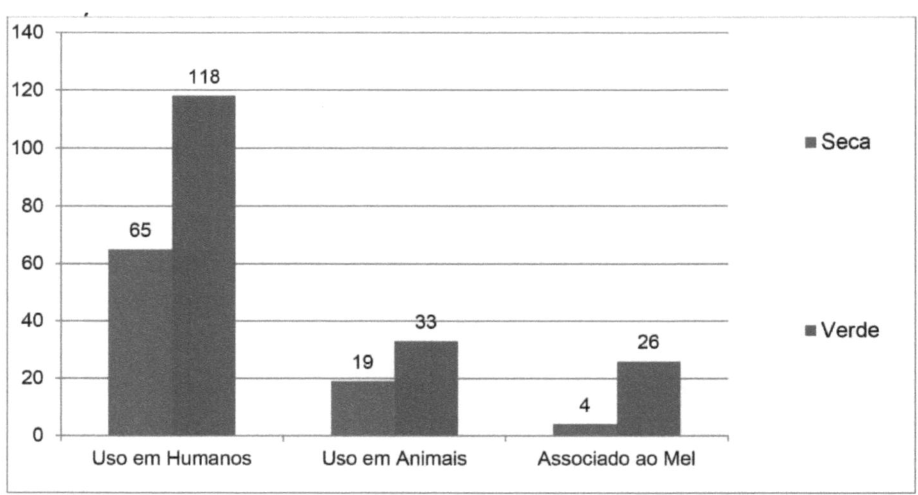


Analysis of the data in Graph 9 shows that medicinal plants are used more in their green state to treat diseases affecting humans. This is also the case when these species are used to treat animals or associated with honey for medicinal purposes in humans, with very little use of plants in their dried state.

A study by Mosca and Loiola (2009) shows that among farmers in Rio Grande do Norte, the most commonly used parts of medicinal plants are the leaves, mainly in their green state.

Castellucci et al. (2000) point out that the leaves are commonly used because they can usually be collected all year round in some regions of the country. They also concentrate a large part of the plant's active ingredients.

Next, we tried to identify the way in which the plant is used by the sample interviewed, i.e. as a tea, gargle, etc. Initially, we collected data on use in humans, which is shown in Graph 10. In this case, we took into account the number of species mentioned, correlating them with the number of participants, i.e. we considered the information given by each participant for the plants they mentioned.

**Graph 10 - Distribution of the sample as to how they use medicinal plants to treat diseases in humans**

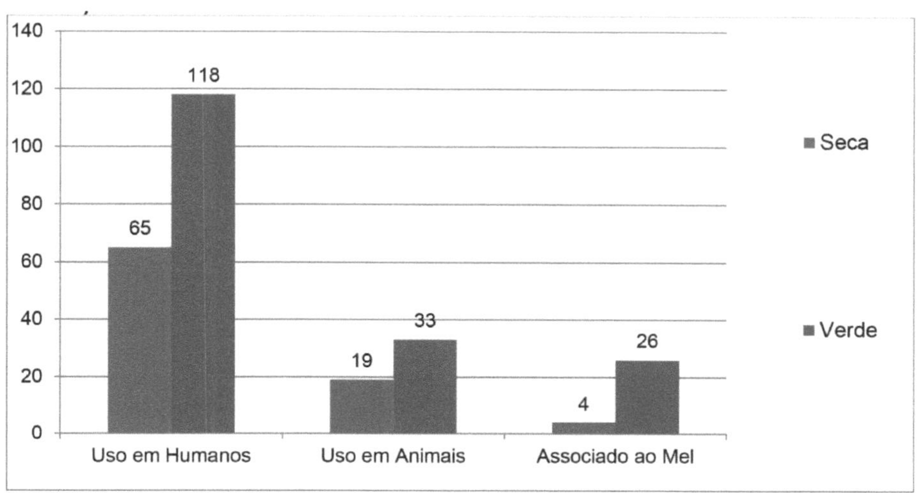


When the data presented in Graph 10 is analyzed, it can be seen that medicinal plants are most commonly used in the form of tea, followed by liquids for drinking and the well-known lick. Analyzing ethnobotany in the backyards of the Abderramant community, in the municipality of Caraùbas, in the state of Rio Grande do Norte, Morais (2011) found that the most commonly used forms of plant preparation for medicines are teas, decoctions or infusions, followed by baths and compresses.

It is important to note that a decoction is the technique of boiling the leaves and roots of medicinal plants. The liquid obtained from this process is used for bathing or drinking.

On the other hand, Marinho; Silva and Andrade (2011) showed that in Sâo José de Espinharas-PB, medicinal plants are most commonly used as lambedor (homemade syrup), teas by decoction and infusion, macerated in water, alcohol, cachaça and wine, sitz baths, compresses and others.

Graph 11 also refers to question nine and lists the data collected on how medicinal plants are used to treat animal diseases, taking into account not the number of participants, but the number of plants mentioned and their respective uses.

**Graph 11 - Distribution of the sample as to how they use medicinal plants to treat animal diseases**

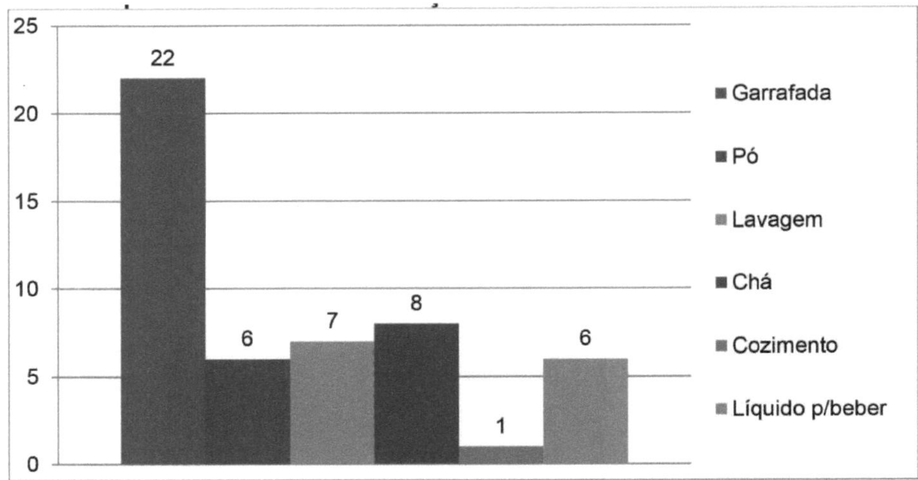



An analysis of the data presented in Graph 11 shows that medicinal plants are most often used in the form of bottles to treat illnesses that affect animals. Tea is the second most common form of medicinal plant used to treat animals, followed by washing, drinking liquid and powder. The latter is applied to the wound to help it heal.

The way in which medicinal plants are prepared for animal use varies greatly according to the region. In Bahia, for example, according to a study carried out by Oliveira et al. (2009), the bark of the aroeira tree (*Schinus terebinthifolius)* is placed in water (infusion) for 24 hours and then given to the animal to drink.

Like the previous graph, Graph 12 is also related to question nine and summarizes the data collected. In this case, the sample was reduced to 28 participants, given that this was the number of interviewees who said they used medicinal plants associated with bee honey (n = 28) and this number corresponds to 62.16%, as shown in Graph 1.

**Graph 12 - Distribution of the sample as to how they use the medicinal plant associated with bee honey**

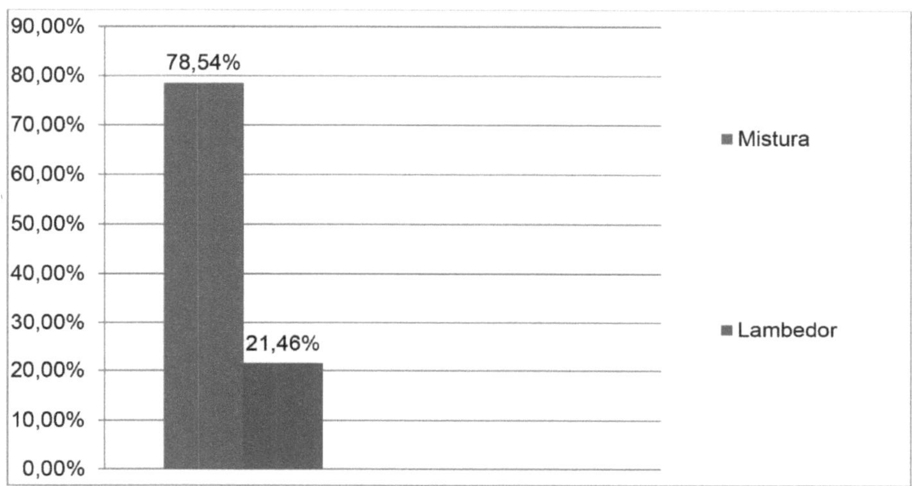


The data presented in Graph 12 shows that the most frequent form of use of medicinal plants associated with honey for the treatment of illnesses that affect human beings is the "mixture", i.e. juice [in the specific cases of lemon and orange] or the leaves, stem or fruit, crushed together with honey, added to milk with a little water [mastruz, mallow, pineapple, mint, etc.]. This was emphasized by 78.54% of the participants who use medicinal plants associated with bee honey. On the other hand, 21.46% of these participants stated that they promote this association through licking, which is produced at home.

A study carried out by Andrade et al. (2012) in Pombal-PB, showed that the homemade lick or syrup is the most common way of using bee honey associated with medicinal plants for the treatment of human diseases in that municipality.

The tenth question sought to find out from the interviewees from whom they had learned how to use medicinal plants to treat illnesses that affect humans and animals, as well as their association with bee honey. The data collected is shown in Graph 13.

**Graph 13 - Distribution of the sample as to who they learned to use medicinal plants from to treat people and animals**

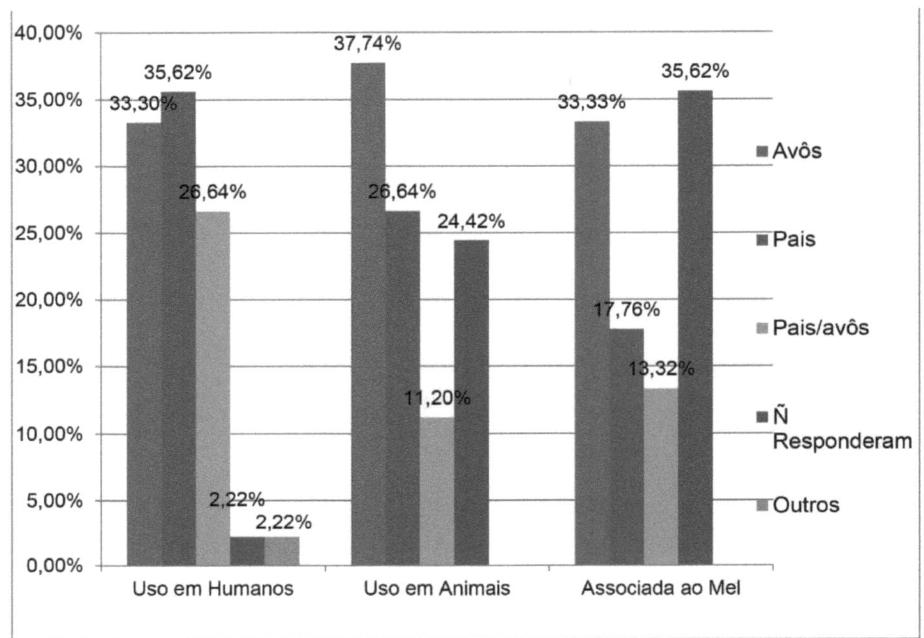

Looking at the data presented in Graph 13, it can be seen that, in general, grandparents are the main people responsible for teaching the interviewees how to use medicinal plants.

However, in isolation, in the case of its use in humans, the largest number of interviewees learned it from their parents, while in relation to the treatment of animals, this knowledge was passed on to a larger number of interviewees by their grandparents, in the same way as occurs in relation to the association of the medicinal plant with honey.

It's important to note that the participants who didn't answer this question were mainly because they didn't use medicinal plants to treat animals and didn't associate them with bee honey.

Conducting an ethnobotanical survey of medicinal plants in a caatinga area in the municipality of Sâo José de Espinharas-PB, Marinho; Silva and Andrade (2011) found that 85% of the people they interviewed said that they learned about the use of medicinal plants from their parents.

These data are quite different from those found in the present study, which also found that grandparents were heavily involved in the learning process regarding the use of medicinal plants, both for the treatment of diseases common to humans and animals.

On the other hand, Guarim Neto; Santana and Silva (2000) show that the use of medicinal plants is strongly present in popular culture and is passed down from parents to children.

Dorigoni et al. (2001) show that ethnobotanical knowledge has been passed down from generation to generation, a fact that demonstrates that medicinal plants are effective in treating various diseases.

It should be emphasized that very often, fathers and grandfathers who use medicinal plants pass on to their descendants not only the habit of using these plants to combat common diseases in humans, but also in animals, always referring to the association of various plants with bee honey for the treatment of some diseases in humans.

In the penultimate question, the interviewees were asked if there were any contraindications to the use of medicinal plants in the treatment of humans and animals, as well as their association with bee honey. The answers to this question were condensed into data and presented in Graph 14. For this purpose, the number of medicinal plants reported by each participant was taken into account, so that some have contraindications and others do not.

**Graph 14 - Distribution of the sample regarding the existence of contraindications when using medicinal plants to treat people and animals**

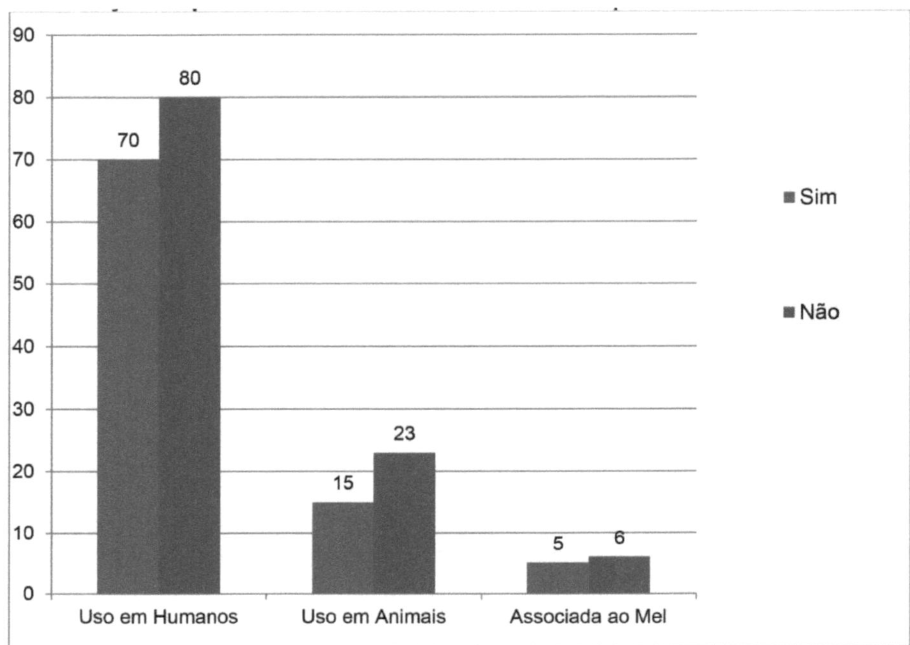


When the data presented in Graph 14 is analyzed, it can be seen that it is in the treatment of human beings that medicinal plants have the highest number of contraindications. However, the participants as a whole listed a greater number of medicinal plants that do not cause contraindications to humans.

On the other hand, when comparing the use of medicinal plants in the treatment of humans and animals, it can be seen that the latter have very few contraindications, and the same is true when they are combined with bee honey.

In relation to animals, Oliveira and Gonçalves (2006, p.39) carried out an experiment in which they demonstrated "an abortive and teratogenic action in animals for the extract of dried leaves and also for the alkaloid boldine".

It should be noted that in Brazil there are few studies analyzing the toxicity of medicinal plants and their use in animals. However, Oliveira et al. (2009) show that some species of boldo are not recommended for use in animal pregnancies, as they have been linked to cases of gastric irritation.

In the present study, fedegoso (*S. occidentalis*) was the medicinal plant most cited by the interviewees, and is widely used in ethnoveterinary medicine. However, Lombardo, Kiyota and Kaneko (2009) show that there is a vast body of literature dealing with the toxic aspect of fedegoso, due to the occurrence of many cases of accidental poisoning of farm animals, adding that the seeds of this plant are pointed out as the cause of the appearance of myodegenerative diseases in animals, causing great economic damage to livestock.

A study carried out by Lombardo (2008) also shows the effects of intoxication with *S. occidentalis* on various species of animals, such as cattle, goats, sheep and pigs, among others. The main effects include liver damage, histopathological changes in the kidneys, degeneration of skeletal and cardiac muscles, weight loss and death.

It should be noted, therefore, that poisoning resulting from the use of medicinal plants in the treatment of animals, when some particularities are not observed, especially with regard to dosage, can have serious consequences.

The last question was to find out from the interviewees which species of bee the honey they use to associate with the medicinal plant comes from.

Taking into account the fact that only 28 people use honey associated with medicinal plants, the sample qualified to answer the last question was limited to this number, i.e. n = 28. The data collected is shown in Graph 15.

**Graph 15 - Distribution of the sample according to the species of bee that produces the honey used in association with medicinal plants to treat people**

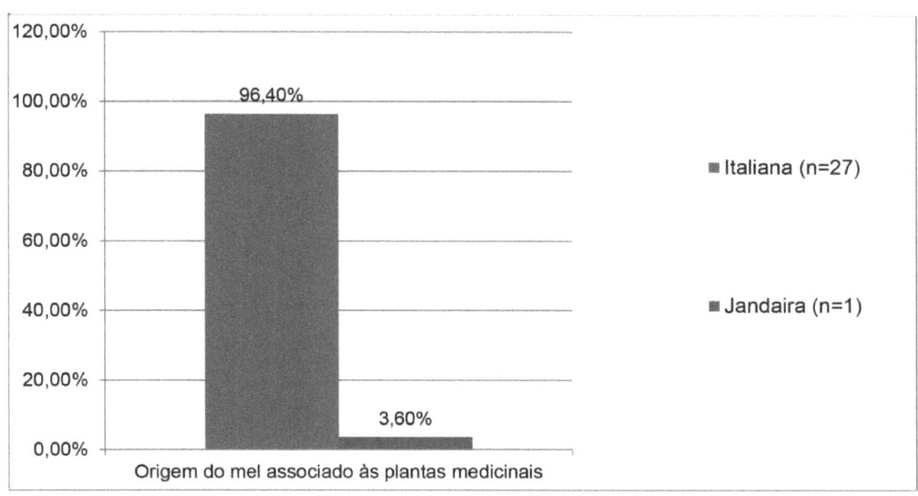


When analyzing the data contained in Graph 15, it can be seen that 27 of the interviewees stated that they use honey produced by the Italian bee (*Apis mellifera* L), which represents

96.4%, while one of the interviewees (3.60%) stated that they use honey produced by the jandaira bee (*melipona subnitida* Duke).

However, a study carried out by Andrade (2012), in the municipality of Pombal-PB, revealed that 100% of those interviewed used honey from the Africanized bee (*Apis mellifera* L.), popularly known as the "Italian" bee, because it is easily found on the market and has well-known medicinal properties. Thus, the results found by Andrade (2012) are in agreement with those revealed in this study.

On the other hand, another study by Câmara et al. (2004) shows that jandaira honey is commonly associated with medicinal plants in the interior of Rio Grande do Norte, taking into account the fact that it is recognized for its therapeutic quality.

It should also be noted that honey from the "jandaira" bee in northeastern Brazil is widely used in the preparation of various home remedies, especially syrups for the treatment of flu and other respiratory diseases.

# 5  CONCLUSIONS

Over 90% of those interviewed use medicinal plants to treat human illnesses and over 60% use this type of treatment in combination with bee honey.

The plants most used by the interviewees were: lemon balm, macela, lavender, holy grass, mastruz and mint.

Most of those interviewed said that they use honey from Africanized bees.

Medicinal plants used to treat diseases in humans were cured by an average of over 90% of those interviewed. When used for animals, they reached an average of 50% and the use of medicinal plants associated with honey reached an average of 48% of those interviewed.

# 6   REFERENCES

AGRA, M. F.; SILVA, M. G. Medicinal plants used as cosmetics in Paraiba (Brazil) and in the literature. **Revista Brasileira de Farmàcia**, v. 72, n. 2, p. 42-44, 1993.

ALBUQUERQUE, U. P. de. **Introduction to Ethnobotany**. Recife: Bagaço, 2002.

ALBUQUERQUE, U. P.; ANDRADE, L. de H. C. Traditional botanical knowledge and conservation in a caatinga area in the state of Pernambuco. **Acta Botanica Brasilica**, v. 16, n. 3, p. 273-285, 2002.

ALEXIADES, M. N. **Selected guidelines for Ethnobotanical research:** a field manual. New York, New York Botanical Garden. 1996.

AMOROZO, M. C. M. The ethnobotanical approach in medicinal plant research. In: DI STASI, L. C. (org.) **Medicinal Plants:** Art and Science. An interdisciplinary study guide. Sâo Paulo, EDUSP, 1996.

. Use and diversity of medicinal plants in Santo Antônio do Levérger, MT, Brazil. **Acta Botanica Brasilica**, v. 16, n. 2, p.189-203, 2002.

ANDRADE, S. E. O. de. **Ethnobotanical and ethnoveterinary study of medicinal plants in the Vàrzea Comprida dos Oliveiras community, Pombal, Paraiba, Brazil**. Monograph (Graduation in Agronomy). Federal University of Campina Grande, Center for Agrifood Sciences and Technology. Pombal: UFCG, 2012

ANDRADE, S. E. O. et al. Ethnoveterinary study of medicinal plants in the Vàrzea Comprida dos Oliveiras community, Pombal, Paraiba, Brazil. **Revista Verde de Agroecologia e Desenvolvimento Sustentâvel**, v. 7, n. 2, p 193-198, Apr-Jun, 2012.

ARAÙJO, F. A. **Ethnobotanical and ethnoveterinary study of medicinal plants in the Jacu settlement in the municipality of Pombal - Paraiba**. 45 p. Monograph (Graduation in Agronomy). Pombal: UFCG, 2011.

BRAGANÇA, F. C. R. de. Considerations on the history of medicines and medicinal plants. In: BRAGANÇA, L. A. R. de (Coord.) **Plantas medicinais antidiabéticas**. Rio de Janeiro. EDUFF, 1998.

CACERES, A. et al. Ethnoveterinary medicine as a tool for comprehensive care of livestock production. In: Congresso Italolatino Americano De Etnomedicina, 13, 2004, Rome. **Proceedings**... Rome: Facolta' di Farmacia, 2004. p. 6-8.

CÂMARA, J. Q.; SOUSA, A. H.; VASCONCELOS, W. E.; FREITAS, R. S.; MAIA, P. H. S.;

ALMEIDA, J. C.; MARACAJA, P. B. Estudos de meliponineos, com ênfase a *Melipona subnitida* D. no municipio de Jandaira, RN. **Revista de Biologia e Ciências da Terra**, v. 4, n. 1, p. 1-10, jan.-jun., 2004.

CARRICONDE, C. **Introduction to the use of herbal medicines in PHC pathologies:** aimed at family health program professionals. Olinda, CNMP, 2002.

CARVALHO, M. G. R. F.; TRAVASSOS, M. S. B.; MACIEL, V. S. Climate, vegetation and soil. In: RODRIGUEZ, Janete Lins. **Atlas escolar da Paraiba.** 3 ed. Joao Pessoa: Grafset, 2002,

CASTELLUCCI, S. et al. Medicinal plants reported by the community living in the Ecological Station of Jatai, municipality of Luis Antonio-SP: an ethnobotanical approach. **Revista Brasileira de Plantas Medicinais**, v. 3, n. 1, p. 51-60, 2002.

COTTON, C. M. **Ethnobotany: principles and applications.** New York: J. Wiley, 1996.

DANTAS, S. A. F. et al. Evaluation of medicinal plants in the fight against bovine mastitis. **Holos**, v. 25, n. 4, p. 92-102, p. 2009.

DORIGONI, P. A.; GHEDINI, P. C.; FRÓES, L. F.; BAPTISTA, K. C.; ETHUR, A. B. M.; BALDISSEROTTO, B.; BURGUER, M. E.; ALMEIDA, C. E.; LOPES, A. M. V.; ZACHIA, R. A. Survey of data on medicinal plants in popular use in the municipality of Sao Joao do Polésine, RS - Relationship between diseases and species used. **Revista Brasileira de Plantas Medicinais**, v.4, n. 1, p. 69-80, 2001.

FARNSWORTH, N. R.; SOEJARTO, D. D. Potential consequence of plant extinction in the United States on the current and future availability of prescription drugs. **Economic Botany,** v. 39, p. 232-40, 2005.

FORD, R. I. **An ethnobiology source looking at the use of plants and animals by American Indians.** New York, Garland publishing Inc., 2001.

GUARIM NETO, G. **Medicinal plants of the state of Mato Grosso.** Brasilia.

ABEAS. 1996.

SANTANA, S.R.; SILVA, J. V. B. Notas etnobotânicas de espécies de Sapindaceae Jussieu. **Acta Botânica Brasilica**, v.14, n.3, p.327-34, 2000.

GUERRA, A. M. N. et al. Use of medicinal plants by the rural community of Moacir Lucena, Apodi-RN. **Biosci. J.,** Uberlândia, v. 26, n. 3, p. 442-450, mai-jun., 2010.

HAEFFNER, R.; HECK, R. M.; CEOLIN, T.; JARDIM, V. M. R., BARBIERI, R. L. **Medicinal** plants used for pain relief by ecological farmers in southern Brazil.

JORGE, S. da S. A.; MORAIS, R. G. de. **Ethnobotany of medicinal plants.** Available at: <www.agrisustentavel.com.divulgamos.htm.>. Accessed on: August 2003.

JORGE, S. S. A. **Riparian medicinal knowledge:** Praia do Poço community, Santo Antônio de Leverger. Mato Grosso (Master's dissertation) IE/UFMT. Cuiabá. 136p. 2001.

LACERDA, J. R. R. C.; SOUSA, J. S.; SOUSA, L. C. F. S.; BORGES, M. G. B.; FERREIRA, R. T. F. V.; SALGADO, A. B.; SILVA, M. J. S. Popular knowledge about medicinal plants and their applicability in three segments of society in the municipality of Pombal-PB. **ACSA - Agropecuâria Cientifica no Semiàrido**, v.9, n.1, p.14-23, jan-mar, 2013.

LIMA, J. L. S.; FURTADO, D. A.; PEREIRA, J. P. S. L.; VASCONCELOS, J. G. . **Medicinal plants in common use in northeastern Brazil.** Campina Grande: CEDAC/UFCG, 2006.

LOMBARDO, M. **Evaluation of the antimicrobial activity and cytotoxicity of aqueous and hydroalcoholic extracts of *Senna occidentalis* L. (Link)**. [Sâo Paulo: Faculty of Pharmaceutical Sciences, USP; 2008.

KIYOTA, S.; KANEKO, T. M. Ethnic, biological and chemical aspects of *Senna occidentals* (Fabaceae). **Rev Ciênc Farm Bàsica Apl.**, v. 30, n. 1, p. 9-17, 2009.

MACIEL, M. A. M.; PINTO, A. C.; VEIGA, V. E. Medicinal plants: the need for multidisciplinary studies. **Quimica Nova**, v. 23, n. 3, p. 429-438, 2002.

MARINHO, M. G. V; SILVA, C. C; ANDRADE, L. H. C. Ethnobotanical survey of medicinal plants in a caatinga area in the municipality of Sâo José de Espinharas, Paraiba, Brazil. **Rev. bras. plantas med.** v. 13, n. 2, p. 170-182, 2011.

MARTIN, G. J. **Ethnobotany: a methods manual.** London, Chapman & Hall. 1995.

MARTINS, E. R. et al. **Medicinal plants.** Viçosa, UFV, 2000.

MASCARENHAS, J. C. et al. **Diagnosis of the municipality of Pombal, state of Paraiba** (Project to register underground water supply sources).

Recife: CPRM/PRODEEM, 2005.

MELO FILHO, J. S. de. **Ethno-knowledge about medicinal plants in the municipality of Catolé do Rocha, Paraiba.** Dissertation (Master's Degree in Agro-Industrial Systems). Federal University of Campina Grande, Center for Agrifood Sciences and Technology.

Pombal: UFCG, 2012.

MING, L. C.; AMARAL JUNIOR, A. **Aspectos Etnobotânicos de Plantas Medicinais na Reserva Extrativista "Chico Mendes".** (Doctoral thesis). Botucatu. UNESP, 2005.

MONTEIRO, M. V. B. **Ethnoveterinary study of medicinal plants with anthelmintic activity.** Dissertation (Master's Degree). Fortaleza: UECE, 2010.

MORAIS, V. M. de. **Ethnobotany in the backyards of the Abderramant community in Caraùbas - RN.** Thesis (Doctorate). Mossoró, UFERSA 2011.

MOSCA, V. P.; LOIOLA, M. I. B. Popular use of medicinal plants in Rio Grande do Norte, Northeast Brazil. **Revista Caatinga**, v. 22, n. 4, p. 225-234, Oct.-Dec., 2009.

OLIVEIRA, F. Q.; GONÇALVES, L. A. Knowledge about medicinal plants and herbal medicines and potential for toxicity by users in Belo Horizonte, Minas Gerais. **Revista Eletrônica de Farmàcia**, v. 3, n. 2, p. 36-41,2006.

OLIVEIRA, L. S. T. et al. Use of medicinal plants in the treatment of animals. **Enciclopédia Biosfera**, Goiânia, v. 5, n. 8, 2009.

PEREIRA, L. R. L.; FREITAS, O. de. **An** evolution of pharmaceutical care and the outlook for **Brazil. Rev. Bras. Cienc. Farm.**, v. 44, n. 4, p. 601-612, 2008.

PONTES, S. M. et al. Use of potentially harmful medicinal plants during pregnancy in the city of Cuité-PB. **Com. Ciências Saùde**, v. 23, n. 23, n. 4, p. 305-311, 2012.

PLOTKIN, M. J. The importance of ethnobotany for Tropical Forest conservation. In: SCHULTES et al.     (Eds.). **Ethnobotany: Evolution of discipline**. New York.

Chapman & Hall, p. 147-156, 1995.

PRANCE, G. T. Etnobotânica de algumas tribos Amazônicas. In: Ribeiro, B. G. (Org.) **Suma Etnológica Brasileira**, v.1, p. 119-134, 1995.

RODRIGUES, V. E. G. **Floristic and ethnobotanical survey of medicinal plants from the cerrados in the Alto Rio Grande region - Minas Gerais.** (Master's dissertation). Lavras. UFLA. 235p. 1998.

SALES, M. F. & LIMA, M. J. A. **Formas de uso da flora da Caatinga pelo assentamento da Microrregiao de Soledade (PB).** p. 165-184. In: Anais da VII Reuniâo Nordestina de Botânica, Recife. Botanical Society of Brazil - Pernambuco Section. Recife, 1995.

SANTOS, M. G.; LOLIS. S. F.; BELO, C. A. Ethnobotanical surveys carried out in two black remnant communities in the Jalapâo region, state of Tocantins. In: PIRES, A. L. C.

S.; OLIVEIRA, R. (eds) **Sociabilidades negras**. Remnant communities, slavery and culture. Belo Horizonte: Daliana Ltda, 2006.

SCHEFFER, M. C.; MING, L. C.; ARAÙJO, A. J. Conservation of medicinal plant genetic resources. In: Symposium on Genetic Resources of the Semi-Arid. Embrapa-Semiârido, **Anais...** Petrolina-PE: EMBRAPA, 1998.

SILVA, A. J. R. **Etnobotânica Nordestina: A relação entre comunidades e a vegetaçao da zona do litoral-mata do Estado de Pernambuco, Brasil.**

Master's dissertation. Federal University of Pernambuco. Recife. 2001.

SILVA, W. W., et al. Action of an alcoholic extract of Capim Santo (*Cymbogon citratus* (DC) Stapf) on sheep gastrointestinal nematodes. **Agropecuâria Cientifica no Semiàrido**, v. 01, p.46-49, 2005.

SOUSA, R. F. Ethnobotanical study of *myracrodruon urundeuva allemao* in the Piancó valley (Paraiba, Northeast, Brazil). **Revista de Biologia e Farmàcia**, v. 7, n. 1, p. 72-83, 2012.

TEIXEIRA, S. T.; MELO, J. I. M. Medicinal plants used in the municipality of Jupi, Pernambuco, Brazil. **Iheringia**, Série Botônica, v. 61, n. 1-2, 2006.

VESTENA, J. G. et al. Utilization of aloe in the daily life of cancer patients. Revista Baiana de Saùde Pùblica. v. 34, n. 4, p. 773-782, Oct./Dec., 2010.

XOLOCOTZI, E. H. El concepto de Enobotanica. In: BARREIRA, D. (Edit.). **La Etnobotanica:** tres puntos de vista y una perspectiva. Xalapa, Instituto Nacional de Investigaciones sobre Recursos Bióticos, 2002.

# 7   ANNEXES

| FEDERAL UNIVERSITY OF CAMPINA GRANDE CCTA - CAMPUS DE POMBA - PB | | | |
|---|---|---|---|
| MUNICIPALITY: _____________________ COMMUNITY: _____________ | | | |
| INTERVIEWEE DATA | | | |
| NAME:_________________________________________ - AGE:__________ | | | |
| PROFESSION: _________________________________ DATE:     // _____ . | | | |
| QUESTIONS | | ANSWERS | |
| | HUMAN | ANIMAL | ASSOCIATED WITH HONEY |
| 1- Do you usually treat yourself or someone else with medicinal plants? | (    ) YES    ( | (    )    YES  ( ) NO | (    ) YES    ( |
| 2- What is the common name of the plant? | | | |
| 3- What disease is this plant used for? | | | |
| 4- When you treat yourself or someone else with medicinal plants, are you cured? | (    ) YES    ( | (    )    YES  ( ) NO | (    ) YES    ( |
| 5- The Treatment Time is: ( LONG OR SHORT) | | | |
| 6- Do you grow any medicinal plants on your property? | (    ) YES    ( | (    )    YES  ( ) NO | (    ) YES    ( |
| 7- Is the plant used cultivated or collected? | | | |
| 8- Which part of the plant is used (root, bark, leaf, seed, stem)? | | | |
| 9- What is the plant's state of use? | (    ) Dry (    ) Green | (    ) Dry (    ) Green | (    ) Dry (    ) Green |
| 10- How is the plant used? (tea, rinsing, gargling, baths, etc.). | | | |
| 11-Who taught you how to use it? (         ) Parents; (         ) Grandparents; (    ) others | | | |
| 12- Are there any contraindications? | | | |
| 13- Which Bee Does This Honey Come From? (Italian, Jandaira, African, Other) | | | |

## I want morebooks!

Buy your books fast and straightforward online - at one of world's fastest growing online book stores! Environmentally sound due to Print-on-Demand technologies.

Buy your books online at
**www.morebooks.shop**

Kaufen Sie Ihre Bücher schnell und unkompliziert online – auf einer der am schnellsten wachsenden Buchhandelsplattformen weltweit! Dank Print-On-Demand umwelt- und ressourcenschonend produziert.

Bücher schneller online kaufen
**www.morebooks.shop**

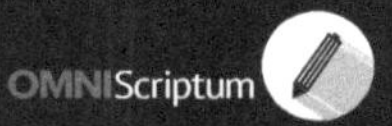

Printed by Books on Demand GmbH, Norderstedt / Germany